# DRUMSET WORKOUTS

## [ Polyrhythms & independent coordination applied to contemporary grooves ]

## By Jon Belcher

FIRST PRINTING AUGUST, 1993
BY IRRATIONAL BEHAVIOR PRODUCTIONS

11247 - 115TH PL. N.E.
KIRKLAND, WA 98033

HAL•LEONARD™
CORPORATION
7777 W. BLUEMOUND RD. P.O. BOX 13819 MILWAUKEE, WI 53213

# ACKNOWLEDGMENTS

Special thanks to Z-PRO in Seattle, Washington, for the patience and expertise with computer work on the drum manuscript, and to Joanie for her help and encouragement.

## DEDICATION

This book is dedicated to Edmund K. Parker,
who taught me the way.

# TABLE OF CONTENTS

# INTRODUCTION

**Drumset Workouts** is intended to help the intermediate to advanced drumset performer achieve a more efficient and complete practice routine. There is so much to learn it can seem overwhelming at times. The exercises developed for this book are designed to organize contemporary drumset skills into a streamlined workout. The workout will help you master and then maintain those skills. By mastering the workouts shown, the player will have achieved an advanced level of drumset coordination skills, and by then **memorizing** these workouts, be able to maintain those skills in practice sessions of modest length. You need time to practice other skills. By applying these skills with imagination in a musical way, the player will then have something solid upon which to build his or her own voice on the instrument.

This book is not a sight reading study. If you need work on reading skills, the Ted Reed "Syncopation" book together with the Bellson/Breines "Modern Reading Text in 4/4" are excellent. The Bellson/Breines "Odd Time Reading Text" is then the logical follow up.

This book is not a snare drum method. If you need work on snare drum technique, learning rudimental drumming (the Haskell Harr Books #1 & #2 are good) and George Lawrence Stone's Book "Stick Control" will help.

# INTRODUCTION

"Drumset Workouts" <u>does</u> begin with some "warmup" exercises (Chapter 1, Exercise #1, Page 6), not unlike the "Stick Control" studies, but is oriented more towards the drumset.

This book offers a practical series of exercises in "drumset coordination" applied to the demands of contemporary styles. In addition to 4-way coordinated independence, I've stressed an understanding of **subdivisions of the beat, polyrhythms**, and **clave patterns.** **Chapter 1**, Example 3, hints at something Indian Tabla players have been doing for years, **subdividing the beat into odd note groupings.** The groups of "5" and "7" shown on pages 8 & 9 are less familiar to the western ear than triplets, but are gradually being assimilated into the working vocabulary for drumset. **Polyrhythms** are an important key to solving mechanical difficulties in drumset coordinated independence, as well as the key to understanding African drumming. **Chapter 2** of this book should help demystify polyrhythms, and **Chapters 3 & 4** offer many applications. **Clave patterns** are the key to understanding Cuban music, but more specific to this book, they will help in understanding the underlying concepts of many contemporary rock and fusion grooves. Contemporary funk grooves use clave patterns in the bass drum line. **Chapter 5** shows the traditional Cuban clave patterns and related patterns, while **Chapter 6** shows their application in contemporary grooves. The drumset, like jazz, is a melting pot of musical influences reflecting cultures from around the globe. Although this book stems from the American jazz and rock traditions, I've tried to incorporate elements of Indian, African, Cuban, and Brazilian drumming. That brings us to **Chapter 7, Triplet Grooves.** Shuffles have been used extensively in jazz, blues, r & b, gospel, soul, country, and rock music. Contemporary hip-hop grooves are really just shuffles felt in 1/2 time. Because they are important to the music of this part of the world, they will continue to be an important area of study for any well rounded drumset performer. Shuffles also represent an aspect of contemporary drumming sometimes overlooked or taken for granted, perhaps because they grew in our own back yard. The most important lesson learned from studying other cultures may be a deeper appreciation for our own.

# DRUMSET NOTATION KEY

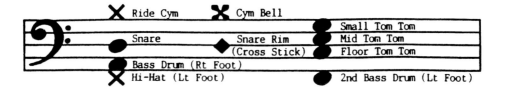

Since each drummer's setup is apt to be different, I have tried to use notation which will apply to most drumsets. Two rack toms, one floor tom, snare and bass drum are now the standard core of most setups, the same setup shown on the cover of this book. The ride cymbal/cymbal bell and hi-hat notation shown are pretty generic, although there will be an occasional note directing you to read the ride cymbal as a hi-hat part played with the hands. In addition, notation for a second bass drum (or second pedal on one drum) played with the left foot is included. Left handed players can, of course, reverse all the sticking and footing notation shown. Since the book is not intended as a melodic study, the player should feel free to re-orchestrate on the kit where necessary as long as all four limbs are still playing the rhythms shown.

# CHAPTER 1

## WARMUPS

**EXERCISE 1:** This is something to warm up the hands. For speed and endurance, emphasize the number of repeats for each measure and keep the tempo brisk. To work on flexibility and control, play the 3/4 measure and the 4/4 measure before repeating, and moderate the tempo.

**EXERCISE 1:**

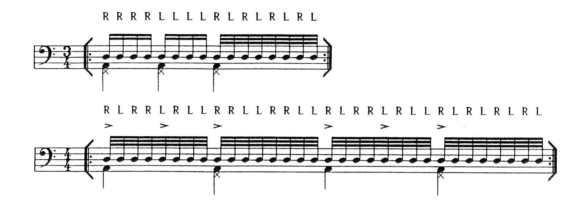

**EXERCISE 1A:** Basically the same exercise using triplets. The accents are shown on this example to emphasize where the sticking switches to left hand lead and back to right hand lead.

**EXERCISE 1A:**

**WARMUPS**

**EXERCISE 2:** This will help warm up the feet especially the bass drum (Rt. Foot). The first measure consists of 5 stroke rolls played with single strokes and substitutes the bass drum for the right hand, while the left foot plays 1/4 notes on hi-hat. The second measure just extends this idea to 9 stroke rolls. The third and forth measures are the same, but the right hand doubles the bass drum on ride cymbal.

**EXERCISE 2:**

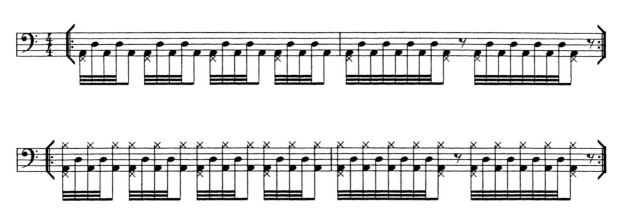

**EXERCISE 2A:** A similar idea with triplets playing 7 and 13 stroke rolls. Play all the warmup exercises in tempo. Straining for top speed is not going to help. Gradually your ability to play at faster tempos will improve if you stay relaxed and focused.

**EXERCISE 2A:**

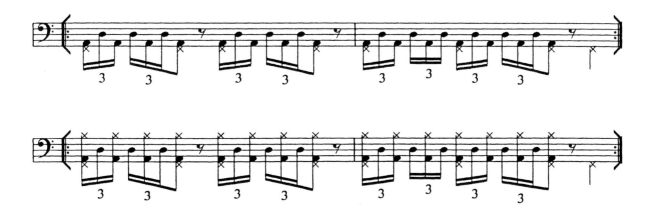

## WARMUPS

**EXERCISE 3:** This is a warmup using the whole drumset. It alternates one measure of time and a one measure fill with single strokes going first clockwise, then counterclockwise around the set. Note that the sticking will reverse when going counterclockwise.

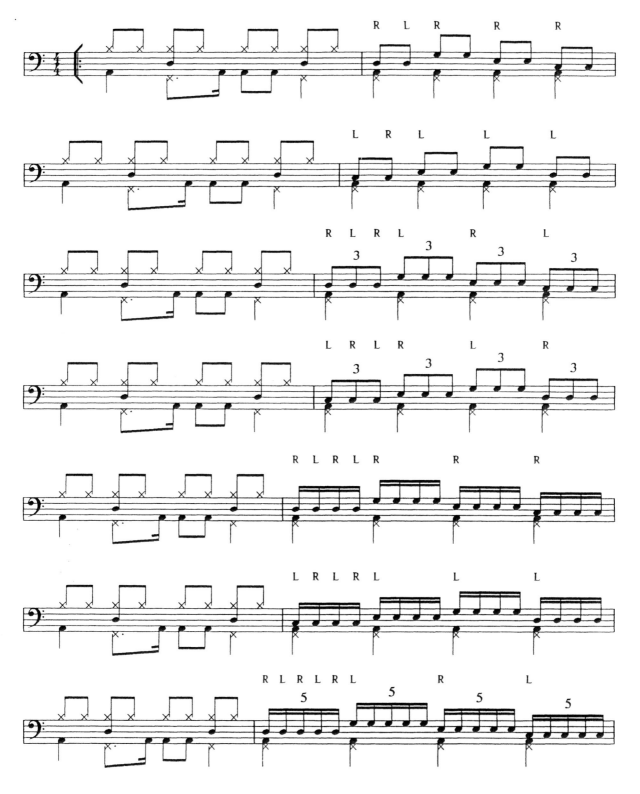

## WARMUPS

Some of these fills became standard repertoire after being
recorded by drummers such as Hal Blaine and Bernard Purdie (two
great drummers and notorious hit makers).  Some will sound a
little less familiar.  Groups of 5 and 7 are useful nevertheless.
If the odd note groups give you trouble, just think of each beat
as a piece of pie and slice it up into evenly spaced pieces.

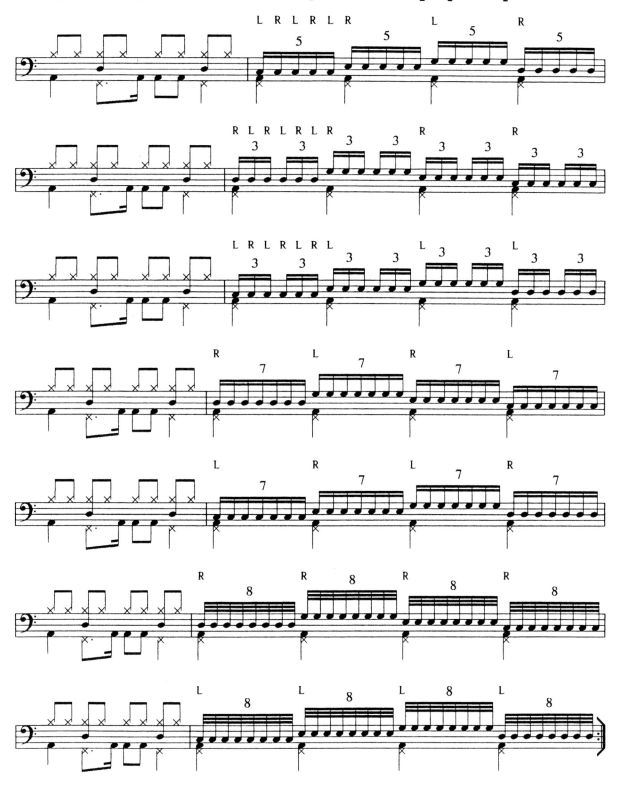

# CHAPTER 2

## POLYRHYTHMS

Polyrhythms are as natural to a West African musician as odd meters are to an East Indian, or syncopation and the backbeat is to an American. One way to look at polyrhythmic relationships is to realize that they are just a way of slicing up time so each polyrhythm takes on the characteristics of a separate pulse. They are separate pulses that cross at regular intervals creating a common pulse.

Let's take a look at the polyrhythms 3 against 2, 4 against 3, and 5 against 4. NOTE: for the sake of clarity, reversing the number (aka: 3/2 versus 2/3) does not change the polyrhythmic relationships, only the notation.

If we take polyrhythm 3 against 2 (example #1), we play 3 notes of one pulse for every 2 notes of the other pulse. It also means that at some point (often on the downbeat), these separate pulses merge. We can notate this as follows:

**EXAMPLE #1:**                    **SOUNDS LIKE THIS:**

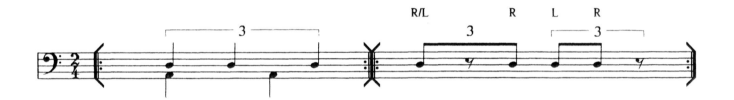

One application of 3 against 2 for the drumset is the African "Nanigo" rhythm. It's usually notated in 6/8 or 6/4, but I've used 4/4 (Example #2) to emphasize the polyrhythm.

**EXAMPLE #2:**

Here the 3/2 cycle repeats twice in each measure with the hands working off the "3" pulse, and feet working the "2" pulse. You see the rhythms merge on the first and third beats of each measure. Bear in mind that you can now improvise off either of the two pulses. This opens up many possibilities for other instruments in the band. Perhaps your bass player is thinking in 4/4 with your feet, and the guitarist is improvising in 6/4 with your hands.

**POLYRHYTHMS**

Next, Example #3 looks at 4 against 3.

**EXAMPLE #3:**

Again, the hands fall together on "1".

**SOUNDS LIKE THIS:**

In Example #4, we have an application of 4 against 3 used as a fill off the shuffle groove.

**EXAMPLE #4:**

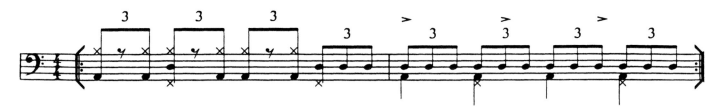

The accents in the second measure played on snare produce the 3 pulse against the 4 pulse on bass drum. The polyrhythmic relationship becomes more noticeable if you accent the bass drum notes too.

Finally, with Examples #5 and #5A, let's try 5 against 4.

**EXAMPLE #5:**

## POLYRHYTHMS

**EXAMPLE #5A:**                          **SOUNDS LIKE THIS:**

NOTE:  Try all the polyrhythms (in Examples #1,#3, & #5) with the hands as indicated, then reversed; with the feet, and finally with hands and feet in combination.  This will give you the coordination to apply them in your own way.  Check to see that each pulse of the polyrhythm is played evenly.  I found it helped me internalize them to memorize the "sound" of each.  A kind of rhythmic ear training.  When you can sing the sound, you'll be able to play them freely.  Try the example #6 groove in 5/4 time.

**EXAMPLE #6:**

The 5 pulse is played on snare drum (cross stick-palm down), while the contrasting 4 pulse is played on bass drum and the cymbals keep time.  Example #6A is included mainly as an exercise to show the mechanics of playing 5 against 4.

**EXAMPLE #6A:**

You'll notice each accent on the snare (the 4 pulse) is spaced five 1/16th notes apart.

## POLYRHYTHMS

In playing situations, try using the polyrhythms to create tension and release it by dropping the emphasis back to the basic groove (home base). If you're worried about losing the rest of the band, try gradually introducing a polyrhythm by bringing the volume up slowly on the counter rhythm, while maintaining a steady pulse with the "base" groove. Also consider the possibility of maintaining one pulse on drums, while others in the band play counter-rhythms to you. In traditional African music all the drummers in the ensemble had their own part or role to play, and it was the interplay between these parts which produced the polyrhythms. A traditional Cuban orchestra operates in much the same way, but with the use of coordinated independence between the four limbs, one drummer can produce these relationships.

# CHAPTER 3

## COORDINATED INDEPENDENCE & POLYRHYTHMS

## ROCK APPLICATION

**EXERCISE 1:** This is something you can use to run through the three polyrhythms described in Chapter 2. It also applies the polyrhythms to a groove which may be used in Jazz, Rock, or Latin contexts. (Think of the tune "Birdland" as first recorded by Weather Report.) The polyrhythms are produced between the left hand (cross stick on rim of snare) and right foot (bass drum). The first three measures use the 3/2 polyrhythm. Measures four through eight use the 5/4 polyrhythm. Measures nine through eleven use the 4/3 polyrhythm. The last measure resolves the rhythmic suspensions with straight eighth notes on bass drum. Note that the left foot plays two and four on hi-hat throughout the exercise. This will help your body find the downbeats.

# CHAPTER 3 (Con't)

## COORDINATED INDEPENDENCE & POLYRHYTHMS

## ROCK APPLICATION

**EXERCISE 1:**

COORDINATED INDEPENDENCE & POLYRHYTHMS

ROCK APPLICATION

**EXERCISE 2:** This is an independence exercise against the basic 1/8th note ride rhythm with the bass drum gradually "accelerating" or closing the subdivisions. The exercise can be played as written or backwards (last measure first). Note the snare on the backbeat with straight 1/4 notes on hi-hat (left foot). Also try this exercise with the snare (left hand) playing the bass drum line while playing 1/4 notes with both feet. Note that measure #1 contains polyrhythm 4/3 between the two feet. Measure #3 contains polyrhythm 3/2 between the feet and 4/3 between bass drum and ride cymbal. Measure #5 contains polyrhythm 3/2 between bass drum and ride cymbal.

**EXERCISE 3:** A similar exercise using the triplet ride pattern. Note that measure #1 contains polyrhythm 4/3 between the feet. Measure #3 contains polyrhythm 3/2 between hi-hat cymbal and bass drum, and measure #6 is polyrhythm 4/3 between the bass drum and ride cymbal.

## COORDINATED INDEPENDENCE & POLYRHYTHMS

### ROCK APPLICATION

**EXERCISE 2:**

**EXERCISE 3:**

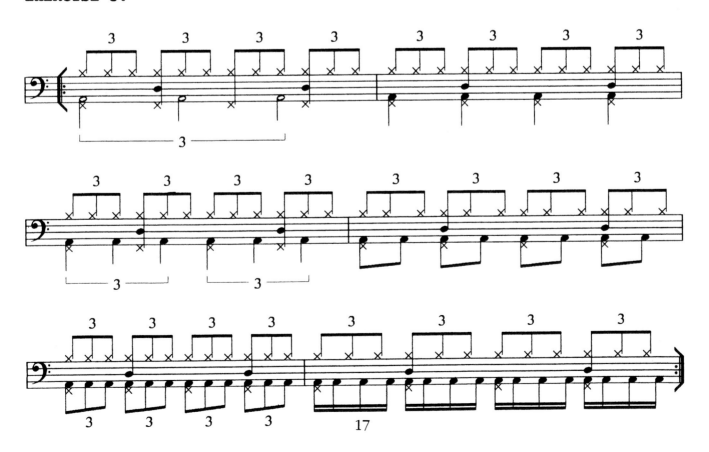

# CHAPTER 3 (Con't)

## COORDINATED INDEPENDENCE & POLYRHYTHMS

## ROCK APPLICATION

**EXERCISE 4:** This one is similar to exercise 2, except that now the subdivisions being played against the 1/8th note ride rhythm alternate between bass drum and snare. The polyrhythms to look for are in the 2nd, 4th, 6th, 8th, 10th, and 12th measures.

The 2nd measure and 12th measure use the 4/3 polyrhythm with the "4" pulse on cymbals and "3" pulse broken up between bass drum and snare.

The 4th and 10th measures use the 3/2 polyrhythm with the "3" pulse broken up between bass drum and snare, and the "2" pulse on cymbals.

Finally, the 6th and 8th measures show the 3/2 polyrhythm between bass drum ("3" pulse) and ride cymbal ("2" pulse).

Strive for accuracy with the exercises in this book. It is not going to feel right unless you start with mechanical accuracy.

## COORDINATED INDEPENDENCE & POLYRHYTHMS

## ROCK APPLICATION

**EXERCISE 4:**

# CHAPTER 3 (Con't)

## COORDINATED INDEPENDENCE & POLYRHYTHMS

## ROCK APPLICATION

**EXERCISE 5:** This is a series of two measure phrases that should start to sound more musical than previous pages. By now you should be familiar with the polyrhythms, but the orchestrations here break up the snare and bass drum into patterns similar to those shown in Jim Chapin's original independence study, "Advanced Techniques For The Modern Drummer". Because rock grooves are often built on eighth notes and jazz grooves on quarter notes, triplet figures in rock tempos are often 1/16th note triplets, where a jazz tempo might use 1/8th note triplets. Note that the hi-hat is played on 2 and 4 during the first measure of each line (while playing time) and stays on 2 and 4 during the fill. This may seem unnecessary, but it does help develop a more balanced and solid time feel.

# COORDINATED INDEPENDENCE & POLYRHYTHMS

## ROCK APPLICATION

**EXERCISE 5:**

21

# CHAPTER 4

## COORDINATED INDEPENDENCE & POLYRHYTHMS

## JAZZ APPLICATION

As mentioned in the previous chapter, Jim Chapin started the whole idea of independent coordination as a way of solving mechanical coordination problems so drummers could better perform the music called "Bop". The drummer was no longer just a timekeeper, but a musician who could join the "musical conversation" being improvised by jazz artists of the time. These next exercises reflect his first book, and also parallel my exercises from Chapter 3.

**EXERCISE 1:** You'll find polyrhythms in the following measures: 4/3 in measures #2 & #8 and 3/2 in measures #4 & #6.

**EXERCISE 2:** Shift the snare line to the bass drum. Remember to keep the hi-hat going on 2 and 4 throughout. Compare both of these exercises to exercise #2 in chapter 3.

# CHAPTER 4 (Con't)

## COORDINATED INDEPENDENCE & POLYRHYTHMS

## JAZZ APPLICATION

**EXERCISE 1:**

**EXERCISE 2:**

**EXERCISE 3:** This exercise parallels Exercise #4 of Chapter 3. Again note that the hi-hat plays 2 and 4 throughout, along with the jazz ride cymbal pattern. Against the ride cymbal and hi-hat, you are breaking up subdivisions between bass drum (rt. foot) and snare (left hand). Keep the volume of your snare and bass drum equal. Also realize that the cymbal pattern should never be overwhelmed by the counterline. Generally with the examples in this chapter you will have to use a lighter touch with bass drum and snare in comparison to what seems normal in a rock or fusion groove. As in all of the previous exercises, the polyrhythms 4/3 and 3/2 are used repeatedly. Don't let the orchestrations or stylistic embellishments fool you.

## COORDINATED INDEPENDENCE & POLYRHYTHMS

## JAZZ APPLICATION

**EXERCISE 3:**

**COORDINATED INDEPENDENCE & POLYRHYTHMS**

**JAZZ APPLICATION**

**EXERCISE 4:** This is actually a twelve bar blues. When writing the exercise I tried to reflect the chord changes of a typical blues with the rhythms. The four exercises in this chapter should also be practiced with 1/4 notes as the ride cymbal line and as a shuffle (reference chapter 7, Exercise 1A). The shuffle patterns shown in this book emphasize the "groove" and not the pyrotechnics, so practicing chapter 4 as an extension of chapter 7 will help round out independent coordination skills.

# COORDINATED INDEPENDENCE & POLYRHYTHMS

## JAZZ APPLICATION

**EXERCISE 4:**

# CHAPTER 5

## CLAVE

Many of the contemporary grooves in chapter 6 (and several in chapter 7) use clave, or clave-like patterns in the bass drum line. They are sometimes embellished, sometimes double timed, and sometimes exactly the same as the traditional patterns. Like the traditional use of clave patterns, they form a rhythmic spine or phrase on which the music is built.

**EXAMPLE #1** - Traditional Cuban "Son" clave pattern (3/2 version). For the 2/3 version, simply play the second measure first.

**EXAMPLE #2** - "Son" clave (3/2) double time notation.

**EXAMPLE #3** - Traditional Cuban "Rumba" clave pattern (3/2 version). This may also be "reversed".

**EXAMPLE #4** - "Rumba" clave (3/2) double time notation.

**EXAMPLE #5** - Two measure variation of the "Rumba" clave sometimes called "Street clave".

**EXAMPLE #6** - Brazilian "Bosa Nova" accent pattern which I will use to function as a clave.

**EXAMPLE #7** - Bosa Nova accents, double time notation.

## CLAVE

**EXAMPLE #1:**

**EXAMPLE #2:**

**EXAMPLE #3:**

**EXAMPLE #4:**

**EXAMPLE #5:**

**EXAMPLE #6:**

**EXAMPLE #7:**

The patterns in the next chapter (Chapter 6) based on the examples shown here, will reference the specific example each is built on. For example, if a pattern is built on the "Son" clave, it will have a ① next to it. If it is built on the double time "Son" clave, it will have a ② next to it, etc.

# APPLICATION OF CLAVE PATTERNS

# TO CONTEMPORARY GROOVES

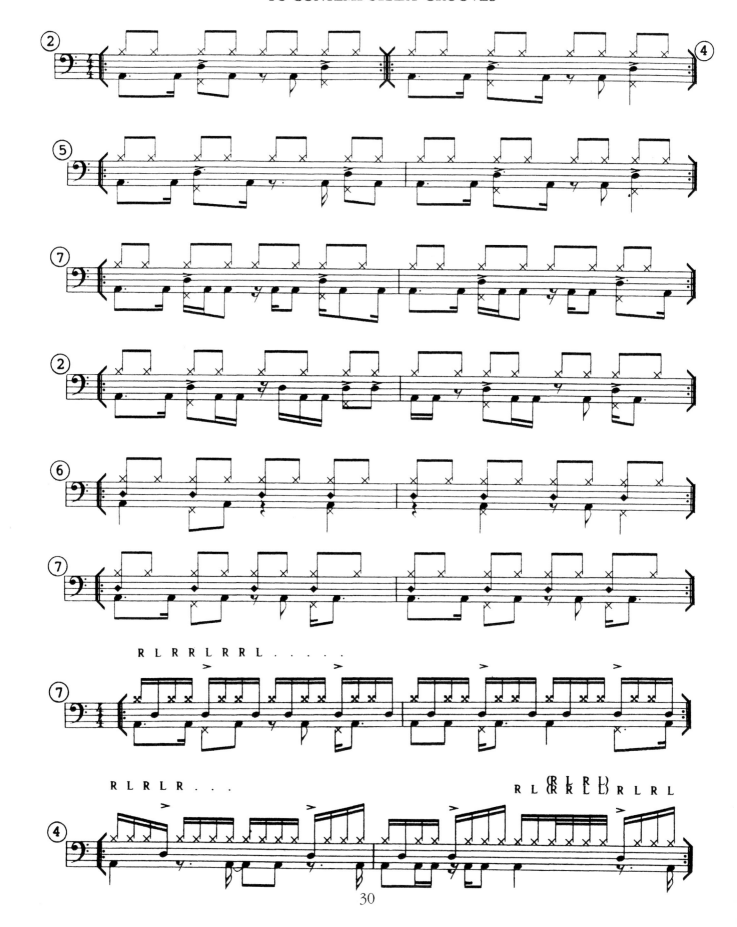

## APPLICATION OF CLAVE PATTERNS

## TO CONTEMPORARY GROOVES

The next groove is a classic example of the "fatback" patterns Clyde Stubblefield and others used with the James Brown Band. While not based on clave, the pattern is included here because it has a very distinctive two measure phrase which functions as a clave. Notice the single paradiddle between bass drum and snare on the third and fourth beats of measure #2.

After playing all the examples as written, substitute the following cymbal patterns.

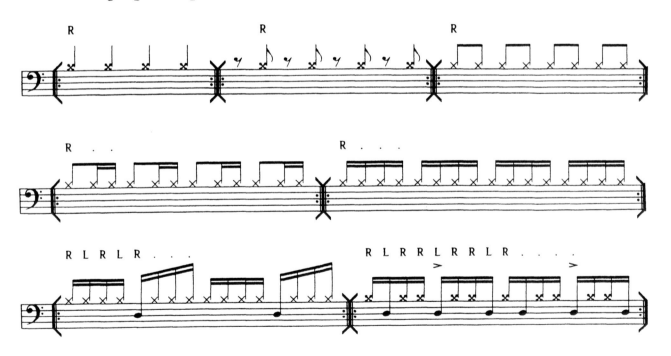

Now try these hi-hat patterns played with the left foot.

# CHAPTER 7

## TRIPLET GROOVES

This chapter came about as a direct result of working in blues, r&b, soul, gospel, country, rock, and reggae bands. The examples look simple after some of the "chopsy" stuff in earlier chapters, but don't be fooled. Hal Blaine, the great studio drumming pioneer, once said "There are really only two grooves you have to know: the 1/8th note rock feel and the triplet or shuffle feel." Everything else is derived from those.

**EXAMPLE #1 and EXAMPLE #1A** are played the same. Example "1" is an older style of notation. We'll use the "1A" notation as a model for the rest of the examples.

**EXAMPLE #2** is a common way to play a blues shuffle sometimes called a Chicago shuffle. The snare doubles the ride cymbal pattern with a rim shot on 2 and 4.

**EXAMPLE #2A, #2B, and #2C** are similar with cymbal variations.

**EXAMPLE #2D** is a common bass drum variation.

**EXAMPLE #3** is often called a Jimmy Reed style shuffle. The bass drum now duplicates the pattern with snare and ride cymbal. This example is also a great technique builder.

**EXAMPLE #4** is sometimes called a Texas shuffle by blues musicians, but it's also used quite a bit by country bands.

**EXAMPLE #5** is a "motown" shuffle also sometimes used by country musicians.

**EXAMPLE #5A** is another "motown" shuffle of the type Larrie Londin was known for.

## TRIPLET GROOVES

**EXAMPLE #1:**          **EXAMPLE #1A:**

**EXAMPLE #2:**          **EXAMPLE #2A:**

**EXAMPLE #2B:**          **EXAMPLE #2C:**

**EXAMPLE #2D:**          **EXAMPLE #3:**

**EXAMPLE #4:**          **EXAMPLE #5:**

**EXAMPLE #5A:**

**TRIPLET GROOVES**

**EXAMPLE #6** - Rock shuffle

**EXAMPLE #7** - a rock shuffle sometimes used in blues bands.
It's a versatile one which sounds good slow, medium, or fast.

**EXAMPLE #7A** - This is reminiscent of the "Purdie Shuffle" or
the 1/2 time shuffle that Bernard Purdie made famous.  Try as
written or on closed hi-hat.

**EXAMPLE #8** - Another common rock shuffle.  This one really
drives the band if you pop those 1/4 notes on the cymbal bell.

**EXAMPLE #8A** - and the 1/2 time variation.

**EXAMPLE #9** - Try using this one like a fill.

## TRIPLET GROOVES

**EXAMPLE #6:**

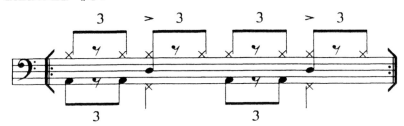

**EXAMPLE #7:**

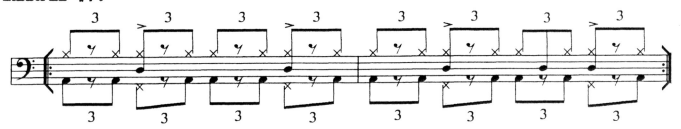

**EXAMPLE #7A:**

**EXAMPLE #8:**

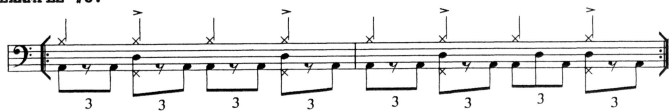

**EXAMPLE #8A:**

**EXAMPLE #9:**

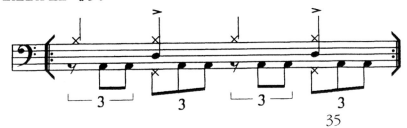

**EXAMPLE #10** - This is a favorite of mine.  The 1/4 note triplets in the cymbal line produce the 3/2 polyrhythm against the basic pulse.

**EXAMPLE #10A** - This 1/2 time is actually a typical 12/8 pattern used for example on a slow blues.

**EXAMPLE #11** - This "fusion" shuffle features two hands on 2 ride cymbals.  It also works well with the same sticking on closed hi-hat.  (Substitute snare on "2" and "4" with the left hand.)  It's very useful when the tempo is too fast for playing triplets with just the right hand.

**EXAMPLE #11A** - and again the 1/2 time variation.  Now the snare substitution is on "3" with the right hand coming off the cymbals or hi-hat.

**EXAMPLE #12** - A rock shuffle for two bass drums.  Try this on closed hi-hat (rt. hand) or cymbal bell.

**EXAMPLE #12A** - 1/2 time with two bass drums; also with closed hi-hat or cymbal bell.

## TRIPLET GROOVES

**EXAMPLE #10:**

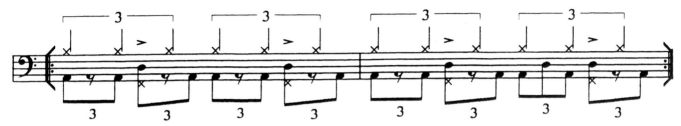

**EXAMPLE #10A:**

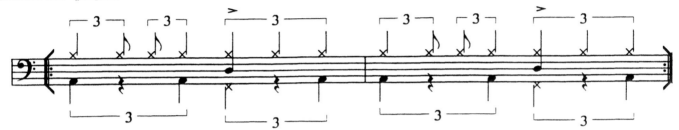

R  L  R  L  R  L  R  .  .  L  .  .

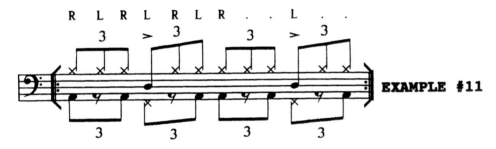  **EXAMPLE #11**

**EXAMPLE #11A:**

R  L  R  L  R  L  R  .  .  L  .  .  .

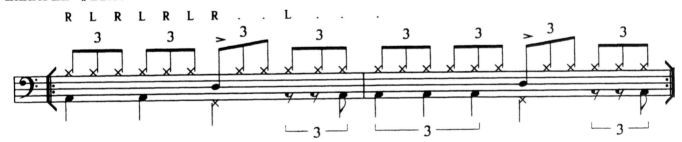

**EXAMPLE #12:**

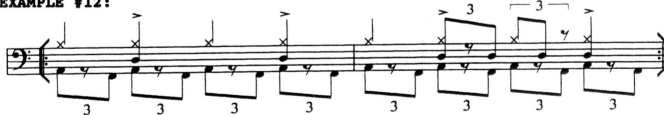

**EXAMPLE #12A:**

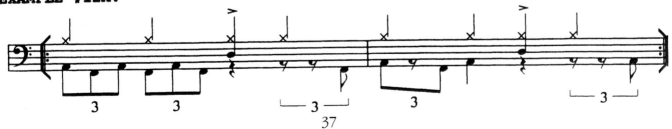

## TRIPLET GROOVES

**EXAMPLE #13** - This is one way to approximate the sound of double bass drums with one bass drum and the floor tom.

**EXAMPLE #14** - "Hip Hop" shuffle. This one sounds good played as written on the ride cymbal, or closed hi-hat (rt. hand). Note:The bass drum line is derived from chapter 5, example #6.

**EXAMPLE #15** - A "Reggae" groove with a "shuffle feel". Play this on the closed hi-hat (rt. hand).

**EXAMPLE #16** - Another "Reggae" or "Ska" groove which is a little more driving. Play on closed hi-hat (rt. hand).

One final note: The 1/2 time shuffles shown are sometimes referred to as "playing on the second line". This is a colloquial expression used by some New Orleans musicians. Think of the original groove as having a backbeat on the 2nd and 4th beats while the "second line" patterns merely shift this accent to the 3rd beat. Although a backbeat is indicated on all these patterns, it can be "implied" rather than played if you want to loosen things up a little. You will not always want the backbeat in a jazz context where the pulse is kept more with the cymbal line.

## TRIPLET GROOVES

**EXAMPLE #13:**

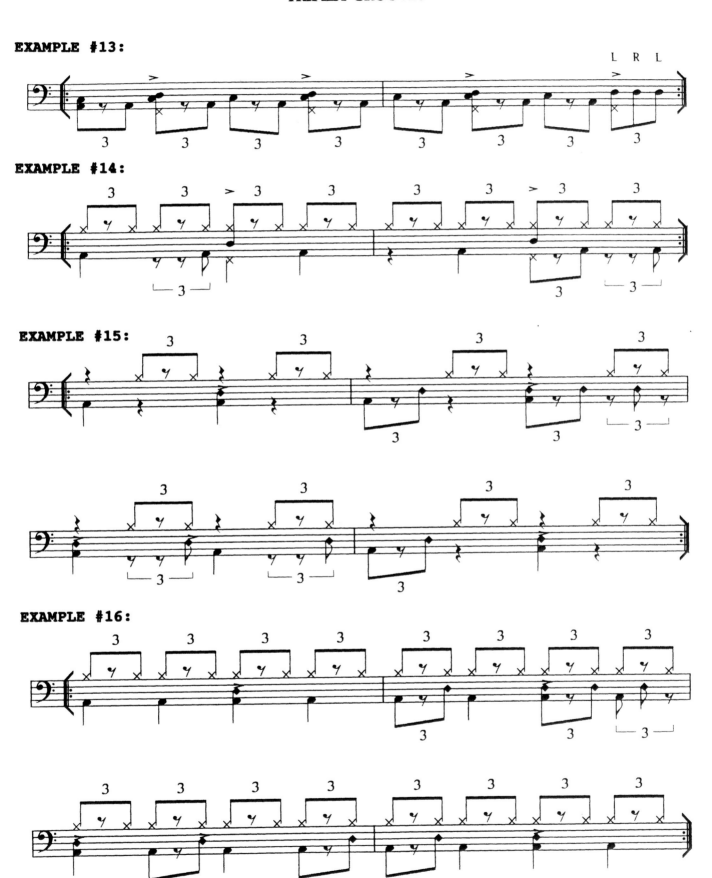

**EXAMPLE #14:**

**EXAMPLE #15:**

**EXAMPLE #16:**

# SUMMARY

**Beginning students** may find this book helpful if priority is given to understanding the underlying rhythmic concepts. The chops and coordination will come if you understand the concepts and you practice. Learn the easier examples in each chapter first, chip away at the hard ones, and find a good teacher.

To the **intermediate level player** this book will present some challenges, but it is very playable, and should give you additional skills that are practical.

To the **professional** the book should offer some new ways of looking at skills you may already have, and help streamline those hours of practice into a more productive result.

# PREVIEW

## BOOK # 2

## DRUMSET WORKOUTS

## FUNKY MOZAMBIQUE

## ABOUT THE AUTHOR

A veteran drummer with over 30 years behind the trap set, **Jon Belcher** majored in percussion at **Berklee College of Music** and studied privately with **Alan Dawson**. His recording and touring credits include **Fat Albert & The Cosby Kids**, **Phoebe Snow**, and **Al Wilson**. He is a drumset clinician and was featured in solo performances at the **World's Fair** in Seville, Spain. Mr. Belcher is currently active playing and teaching drums in the Seattle area.